Reading Success Mini-Books

WORD FAMILIES

Twenty Interactive Mini-Books That Help Every Child Get a Great Start in Reading

by Mary Beth Spann

SCHOLASTIC

PROFESSIONAL BOOKS

New York ● Toronto ● London ● Auckland ● Sydney ● Mexico City ● New Delhi ● Hong Kong

Cover design by Jaime Lucero

Interior design by Ellen Matlach Hassell
for Boultinghouse & Boultinghouse, Inc.

Illustrations by James Graham Hale

ISBN: 0-439-10439-4

Contents

Introduction

The Mini-Books

Introduction

Welcome to *Reading Success Mini-Books: Word Families*. This book provides a fun and easy way for young children to experience simple rhyming words. Beginning readers will really benefit from completing and collecting all 20 of these little books. When used as a regular part of a balanced approach to literacy—one that includes reading, writing, speaking, and listening—the books will provide children with an easy-to-understand, concrete foundation for rhyming word family mastery.

Research tells us that children learn letter sounds best when they're presented in a meaningful context. Each rhyming word family mini-book, introduces a group of simple, illustrated words that feature the same-sounding word ending. Each mini-book offers children the chance to practice writing and reading these rhyming words, and provides a simple review activity so children can test themselves on what they've learned.

The books' small size means they are a breeze for young students to complete, store, collect, and keep. They help give children a sense of mastery and ownership over the letter sounds and words they are learning. In a way, these mini-books serve as children's own print-awareness progress reports. As children successfully work through the books, it's easy for them to see how each one represents an important step on the road to reading.

Assembling the Mini-Books

1. Make a double-sided copy of the mini-book pages.

2. Cut the page in half along the solid line.

3. Place pages 4/5 on top of pages 2/7 as shown.

4. Fold the pages in half along the dotted line.

5. Check to be sure that the pages are in the proper order and then staple them together along the book's spine.

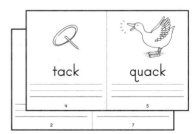

How to Use This Book

This book contains 20 rhyming mini-books representing 20 different common rhyming word endings. How you introduce and share these books with children will largely depend on how you introduce rhyming sounds and word endings in general. But no matter how you choose to use them, you'll find these mini-books to be small but powerful page-turners. Here are some ideas for putting them to work in your classroom:

Pre-assemble Mini-Books as Needed

Instead of asking children to assemble these books in class, you may want to assemble a complete class set ahead of time. This prep-step allows students to focus their attention on the mini-books' content, rather than on construction. Remember: Parents who are unable to volunteer in the classroom may welcome this task as something they can work on at home.

Let the Books Serve You

Here are some quick tips for making the mini-books a successful part of your reading routine:

- If you prefer whole-class instruction—at least for your introductory lessons—you may choose to have each student, or small groups of students, work on the same word-family mini-book simultaneously.

- For a more individualized approach, in which each child explores rhymes at his or her own rate, you may make the books available to children on an "as-needed" basis. Perhaps you can set up a rhyme-time learning center, stocked with a supply of mini-books in numbered envelopes. When individualizing, keep a mini-book checklist showing which ones each child has completed. Be certain to schedule student/teacher conferences so you can assess and celebrate children's progress.

- As children learn how to read and spell the words in the books, consider transferring the words to word wall lists. Invite children to write and illustrate additional words for each list. Encourage children to refer to their mini-books and/or word walls when writing stories and books of their own.

Recommended Read

In his comprehensive resource book, *Phonics From A to Z: A Practical Guide* (Scholastic Professional Books, 1998), reading expert Wiley Blevins recommends a phonics sequence for introducing letters and sounds. Because this must-have book offers explanations and rationales for all aspects of phonics instruction, it is very helpful in guiding the use of phonics mini-books.

Introducing the Mini-Books in Class

1. Show children how a book is constructed and what they are expected to do on each page.

2. Work through one mini-book together.

   a. Read the cover together. Demonstrate how to use the "Name" line. Call attention to the configuration of the letters printed there.

   b. Call attention to the picture and word on each page. When children correctly identify a picture by reading the word, invite them to explain their reading strategies. In doing so, you are asking children to pay attention to the print features of the word below the picture.

   c. Demonstrate how to copy the word on the line provided. Suggest to children that if they think they already know how to spell the word, they can try and cover the word below the picture and write the word without peeking.

   d. Show how the back-cover activity serves as a self-checking review page. (Tip: The back cover can also serve as a screening page. If you suspect a child already knows how to read, spell, and write all the words in a mini-book, you can ask him or her to complete this page before completing the whole book. That way you'll know if the child needs to move on to a mini-book that is at a more appropriate instructional level.)

Mini-Book Extensions

- Meet periodically with each student to review mini-books together. To organize their mini-book collections, give each child a large metal loose-leaf ring. Punch a hole in the upper left-hand corner of each completed mini-book and slip each one onto the ring. Store collections in a multi-pocketed shoe bag (hanging on the wall or from a door-knob), or hung on wall hooks.

- A tree trunk and branches decorated with a few paper leaves makes a nice bulletin board backdrop for displaying new books (before adding them to the rings). Just tack individual books to the branches so they resemble leaves. Title your display "Leaf Through a Mini-Book!"

- Set aside class time for children to take turns sharing one book of their choice.

- Designate one day a week as "Mini-Book Take-Home Day" so children can share their growing library with family members.

- Provide blank mini-books so children can write and illustrate their own rhyming-word collections. Have children compile books of real and/or silly rhyming words.

Generating Family Support

1. When familiarizing families with instructional materials and strategies you plan on using to teach reading and writing, introduce phonics mini-books as part of your overall approach.

2. Emphasize that a well-balanced program includes phonics plus many other strategies for reading, speaking, listening, and writing with children. Share specific examples of how you include these components in your program.

3. Invite families to extend learning at home by reading aloud together every day, by calling attention to any written material that fills their days, and by reviewing school work—including mini-books—with their children.

Add a letter or letters to make a real or silly rhyming word. Draw a picture to go with it.

_____ ack

8

My Book of Words Ending in
ack

Name _____

1

stack

6

pack

3

back

2

track

7

tack

4

quack

5

Add a letter or letters to make a real or silly rhyming word. Draw a picture to go with it.

_____

ag

8

Reading Success Mini-Books: Word Families Scholastic Professional Books

Name _____

1

flag

_____

6

rag

_____

3

bag

2

snag

7

tag

4

wag

5

Add a letter or letters to make a real or silly rhyming word. Draw a picture to go with it.

Reading Success Mini-Books: Word Families   Scholastic Professional Books

My Book of Words Ending in
ail

Name _____

ail

snail

mail

hail

2

tail

7

nail

4

pail

5

Add a letter or letters to make a real or silly rhyming word. Draw a picture to go with it.

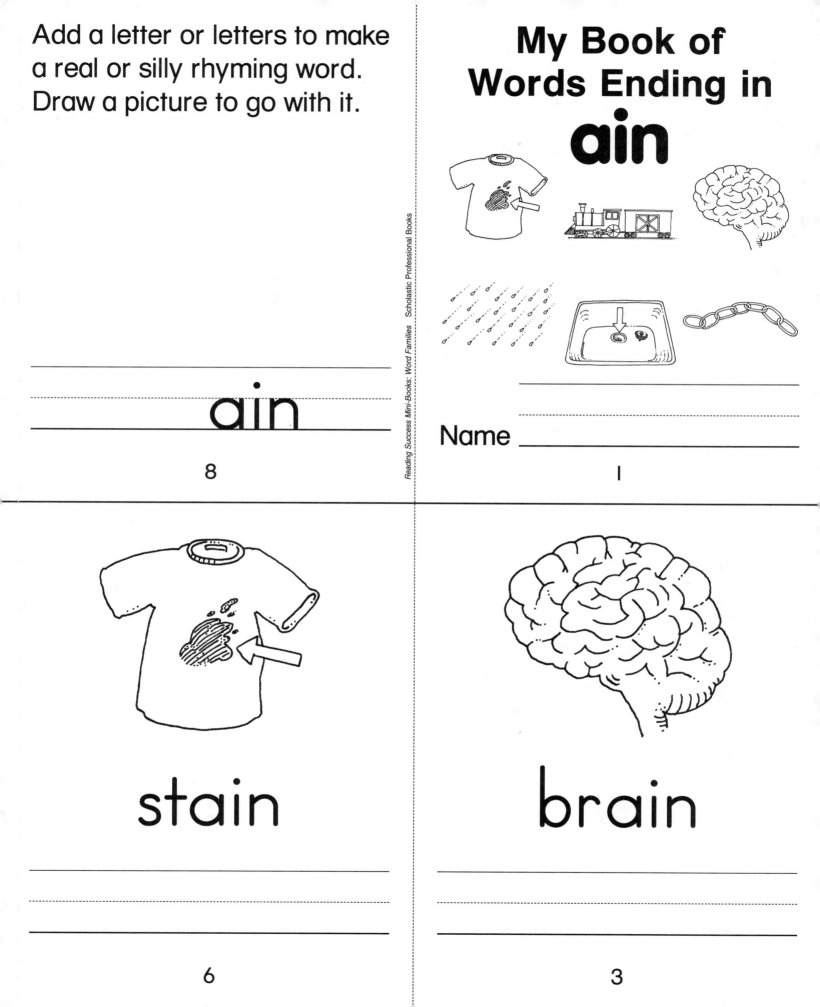

ain

8

Reading Success Mini-Books: Word Families   Scholastic Professional Books

My Book of Words Ending in
ain

Name _____

1

stain

6

brain

3

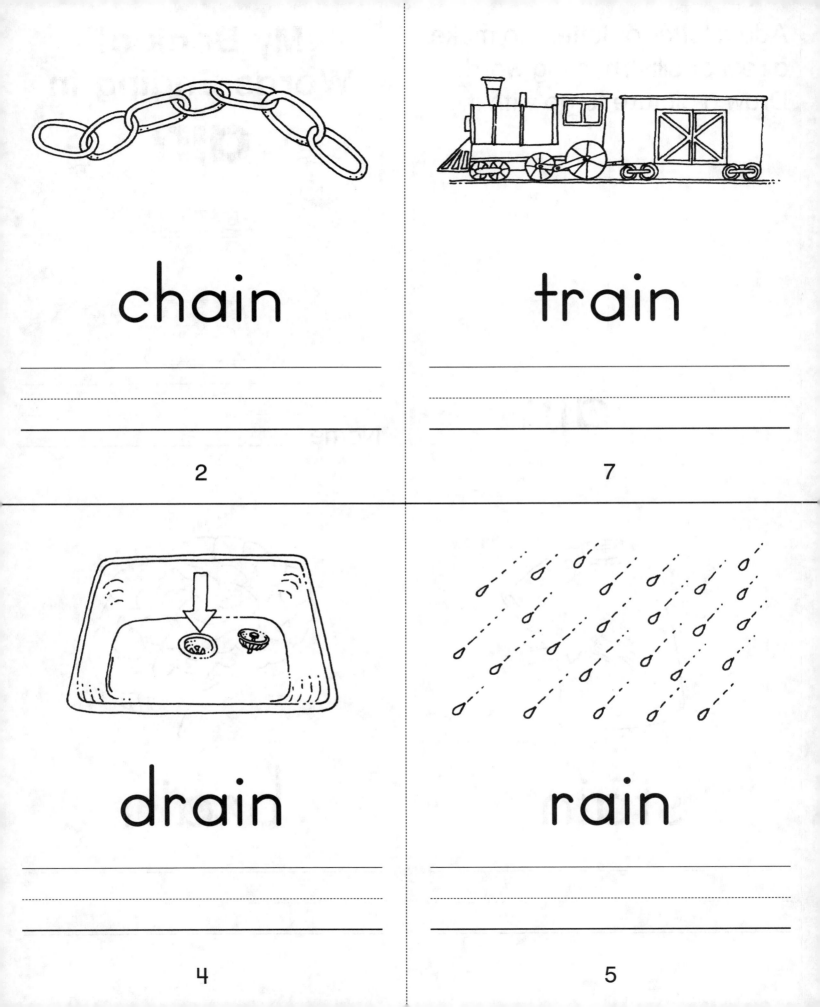

chain

2

train

7

drain

4

rain

5

Add a letter or letters to make a real or silly rhyming word. Draw a picture to go with it.

ake

8

Reading Success Mini-Books: Word Families   Scholastic Professional Books

Name _____

1

snake

6

lake

3

cake

2

stake

7

rake

4

flake

5

Add a letter or letters to make a real or silly rhyming word. Draw a picture to go with it.

_____
- - - - - - - - - - - - - - - - - -
am
_____

8

Reading Success Mini-Books: Word Families   Scholastic Professional Books

My Book of Words Ending in
am

_____
- - - - - - - - - - - - - - - - - -
Name _____

1

clam

_____
- - - - - - - - - - - - - - - - - -
_____

6

dam

_____
- - - - - - - - - - - - - - - - - -
_____

3

jam

2

swam

7

ham

4

ram

5

Add a letter or letters to make a real or silly rhyming word. Draw a picture to go with it.

_____

an

8

My Book of Words Ending in

an

_____

Name _____

1

Reading Success Mini-Books: Word Families   Scholastic Professional Books

man

_____

6

ran

_____

3

can

2

van

7

fan

4

pan

5

Add a letter or letters to make
a real or silly rhyming word.
Draw a picture to go with it.

ane

8

Reading Success Mini-Books: Word Families   Scholastic Professional Books

Name _____

1

vane

6

crane

3

cane

2

plane

7

mane

4

pane

5

Add a letter or letters to make a real or silly rhyming word. Draw a picture to go with it.

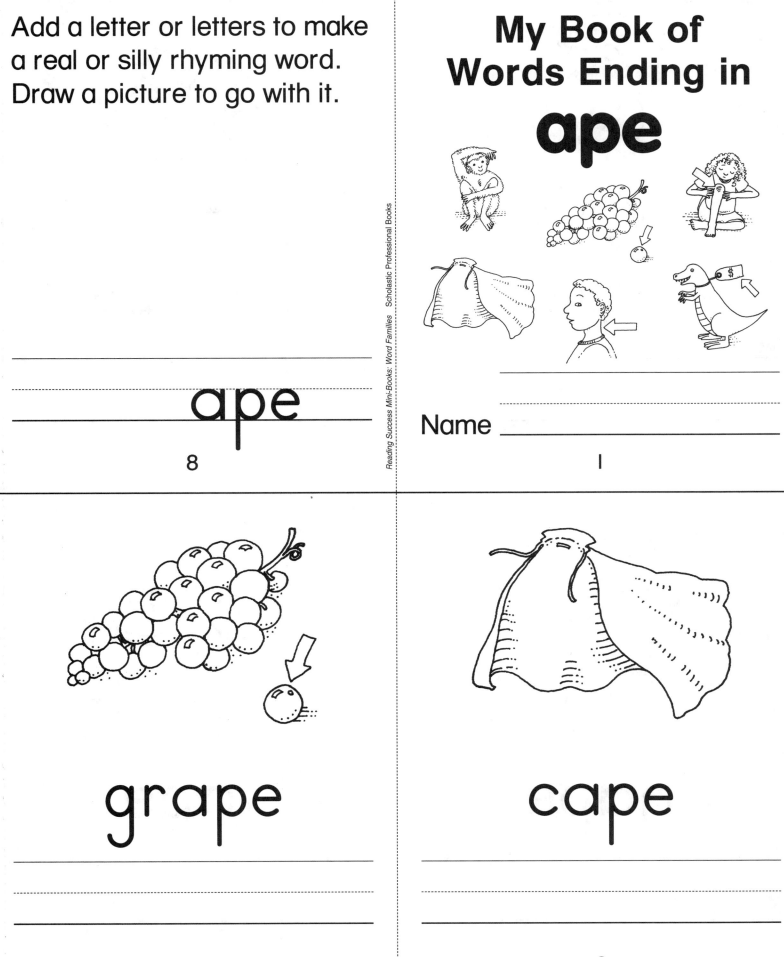

ape

8

My Book of Words Ending in
ape

Name _____

1

grape

6

cape

3

Reading Success Mini-Books: Word Families   Scholastic Professional Books

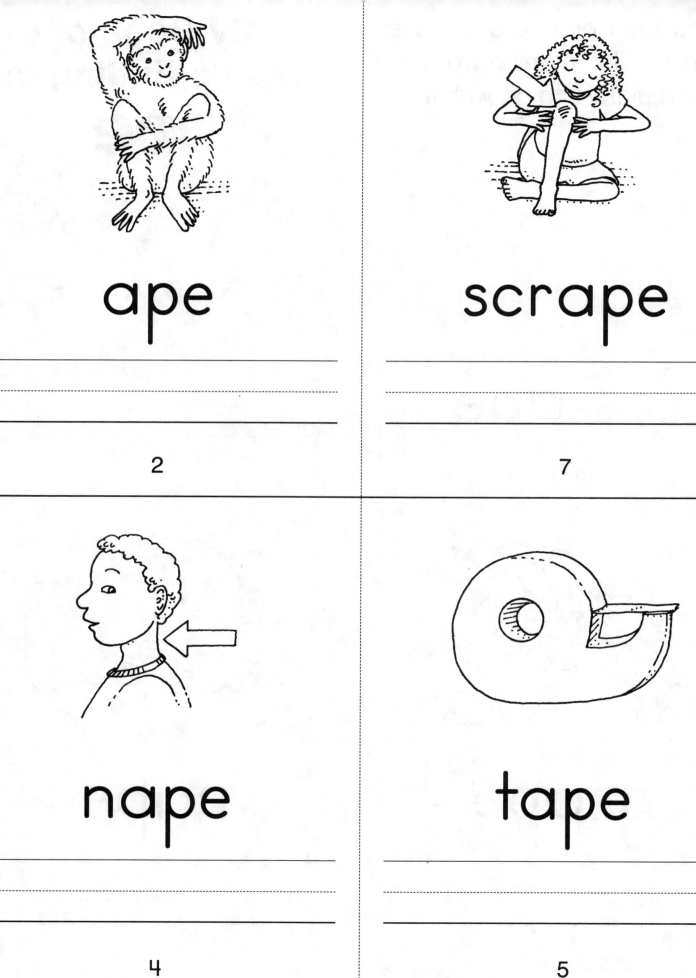

ape

2

scrape

7

nape

4

tape

5

Add a letter or letters to make a real or silly rhyming word. Draw a picture to go with it.

_____

ay

8

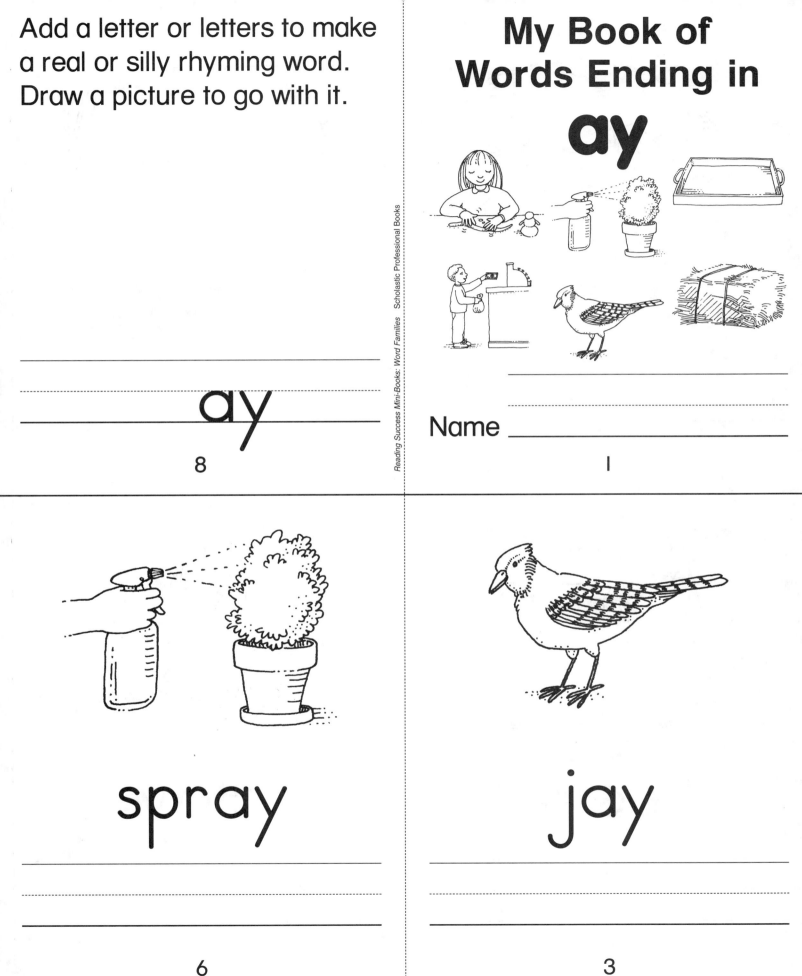

Name _____

1

Reading Success Mini-Books: Word Families   Scholastic Professional Books

spray

6

jay

3

hay

2

tray

7

pay

4

clay

5

Add a letter or letters to make a real or silly rhyming word. Draw a picture to go with it.

ell

8

My Book of Words Ending in
ell

Reading Success Mini-Books: Word Families   Scholastic Professional Books

Name _____

1

yell

6

fell

3

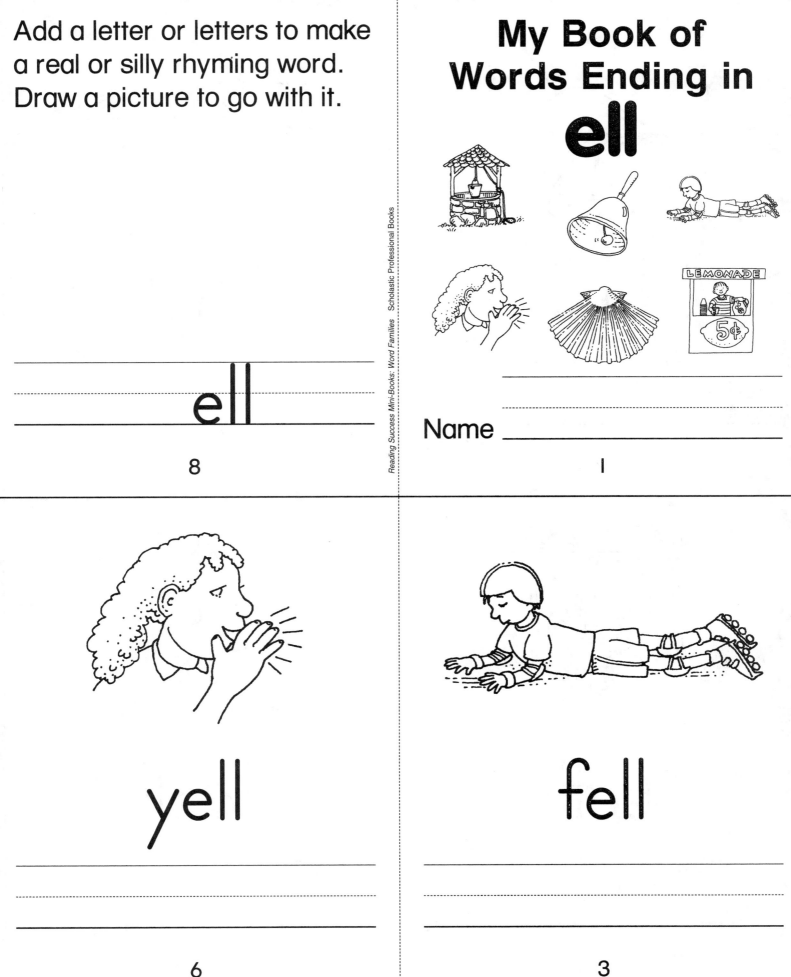

bell

2

shell

7

sell

4

well

5

Add a letter or letters to make a real or silly rhyming word. Draw a picture to go with it.

ill

8

My Book of Words Ending in
ill

Reading Success Mini-Books: Word Families   Scholastic Professional Books

Name _____

1

drill

6

bill

3

ill

2

grill

7

hill

4

pill

5

Add a letter or letters to make a real or silly rhyming word. Draw a picture to go with it.

_____
ing

8

My Book of Words Ending in
ing

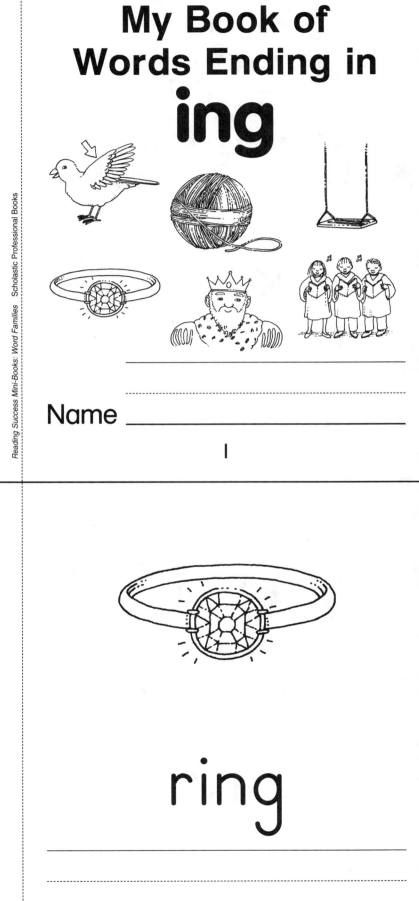

Name _____

1

string

6

ring

3

king

2

swing

7

sing

4

wing

5

Add a letter or letters to make a real or silly rhyming word. Draw a picture to go with it.

ink

8

My Book of Words Ending in ink

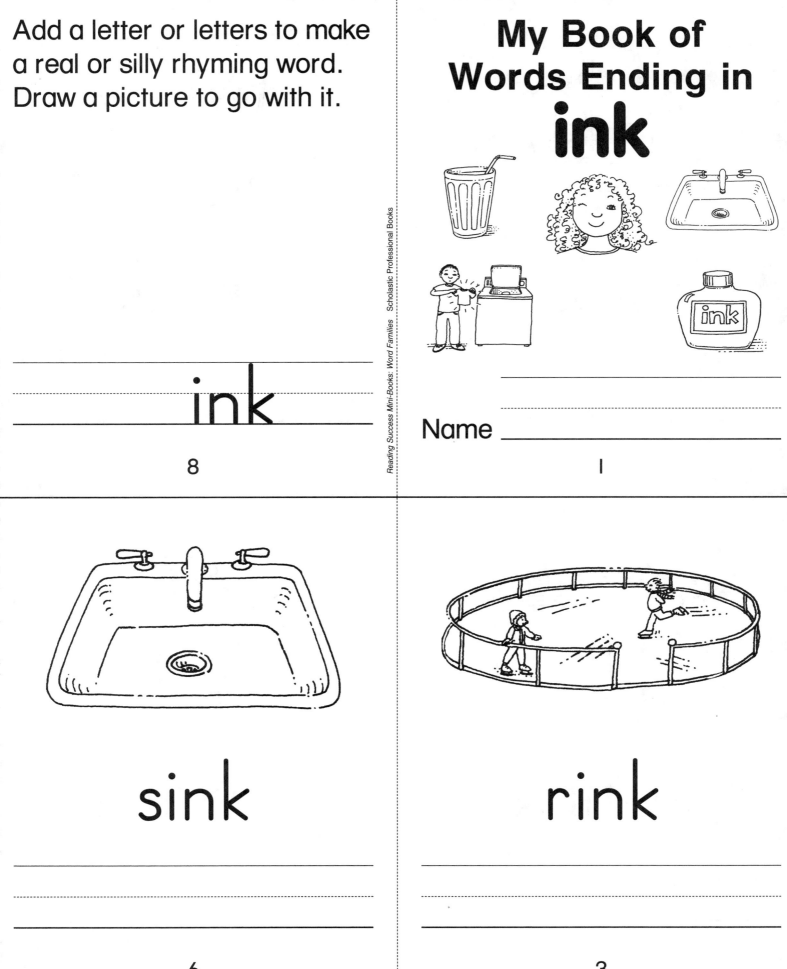

Name _____

1

Reading Success Mini-Books: Word Families   Scholastic Professional Books

sink

6

rink

3

ink

2

drink

7

shrink

4

wink

5

Add a letter or letters to make a real or silly rhyming word. Draw a picture to go with it.

_____
ip
_____

8

My Book of Words Ending in
ip

_____
Name _____

Reading Success Mini-Books: Word Families Scholastic Professional Books

1

tip

_____
_____

6

hip

_____
_____

3

dip

2

flip

7

lip

4

rip

5

Add a letter or letters to make
a real or silly rhyming word.
Draw a picture to go with it.

_____ ock

8

Reading Success Mini-Books: Word Families   Scholastic Professional Books

My Book of Words Ending in
ock

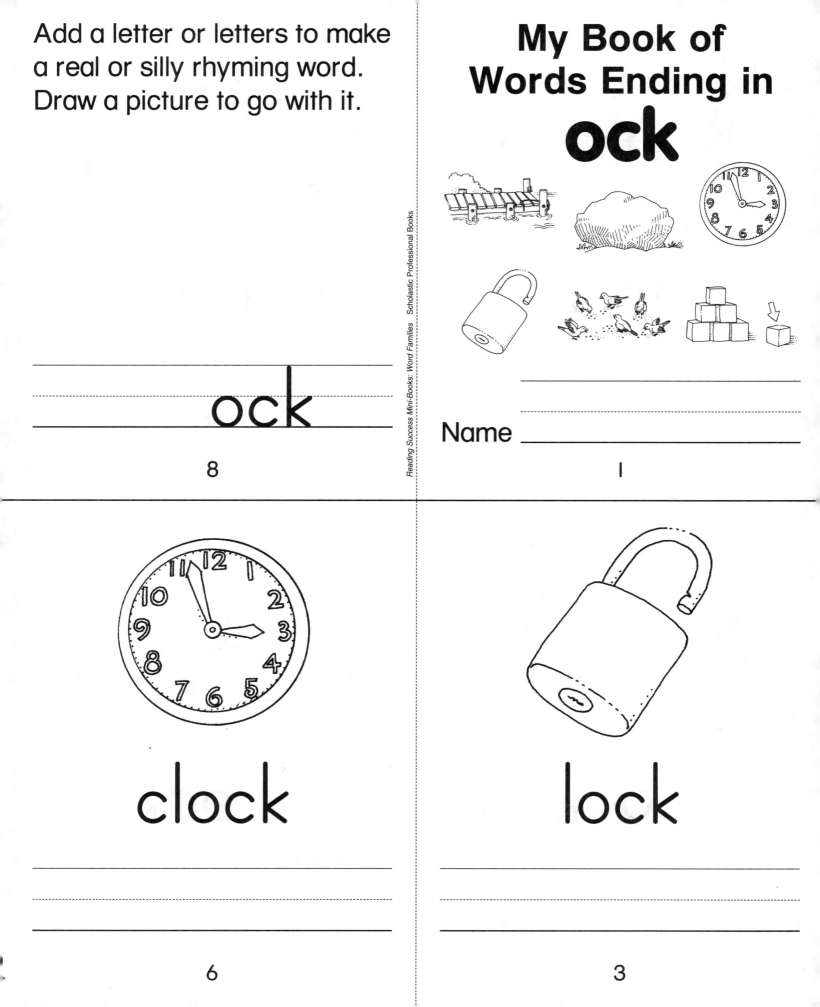

Name _____

I

clock

6

lock

3

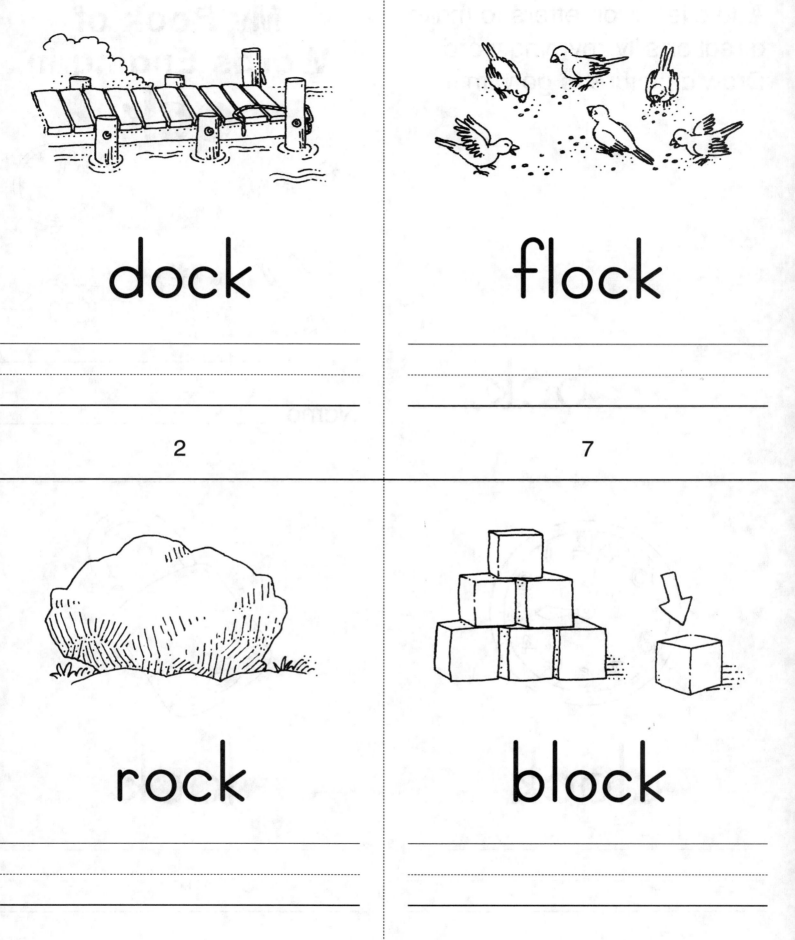

dock

2

flock

7

rock

4

block

5

Add a letter or letters to make a real or silly rhyming word. Draw a picture to go with it.

_____

_____ op _____

8

Reading Success Mini-Books: Word Families   Scholastic Professional Books

Name _____

1

top

_____

6

hop

_____

3

cop

2

stop

7

mop

4

pop

5

Add a letter or letters to make a real or silly rhyming word. Draw a picture to go with it.

own

8

Reading Success Mini-Books: Word Families   Scholastic Professional Books

My Book of Words Ending in
OWN

Name _____

1

clown

6

gown

3

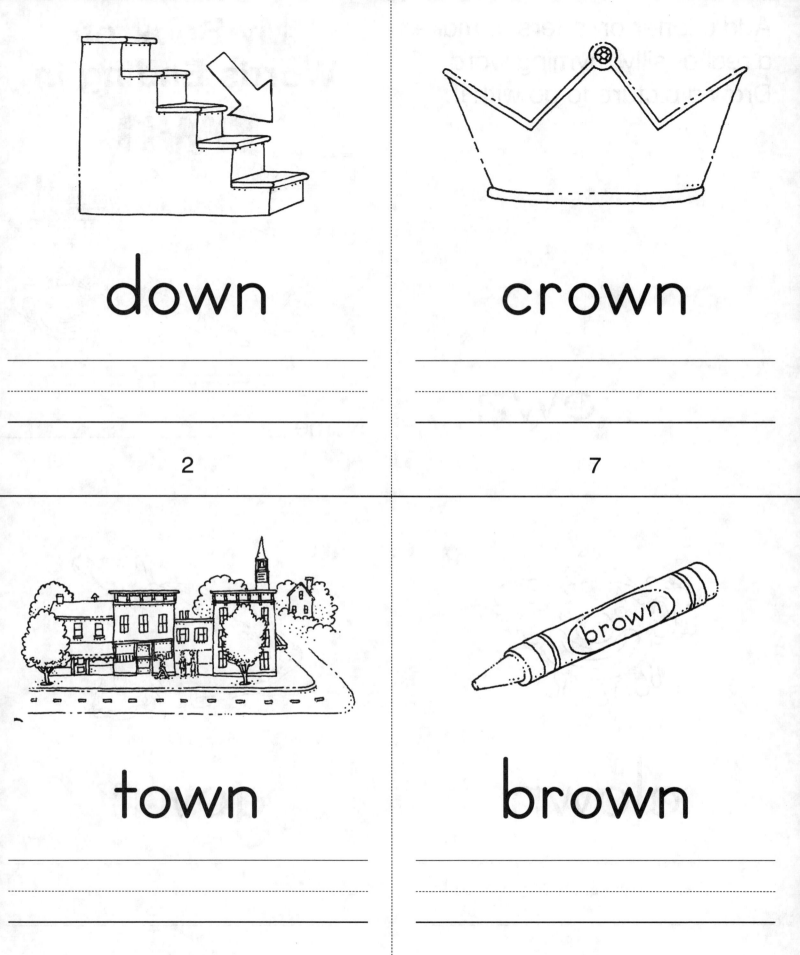

down

2

crown

7

town

4

brown

5

Add a letter or letters to make a real or silly rhyming word. Draw a picture to go with it.

_____ ug

8

My Book of Words Ending in
ug

Name _____

I

rug

6

hug

3

bug

tug

jug

mug

Add a letter or letters to make a real or silly rhyming word. Draw a picture to go with it.

_____

ump

8

My Book of Words Ending in
ump

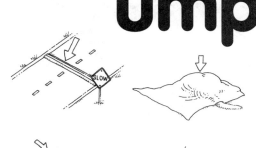

Name _____

1

Reading Success Mini-Books: Word Families   Scholastic Professional Books

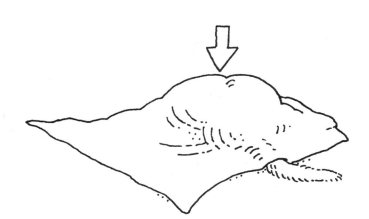

lump

_____

6

dump

_____

3

bump

2

pump

7

hump

4

jump

5